MW01059062

# *An Advent Pilgrimage*

Preparing Our Hearts for Jesus

# An Advent Pilgrimage

## Preparing Our Hearts for Jesus

*By Archbishop J. Peter Sartain*

Our Sunday Visitor Publishing Division
Our Sunday Visitor, Inc.
Huntington, Indiana 46750

Copyright © 2014 by Archbishop J. Peter Sartain. Published 2014.

20 19 18 17 16 15 14     1 2 3 4 5 6 7 8 9

ISBN: 978-1-61278-865-4 (Inventory No. X1579)
eISBN: 978-1-61278-864-7

Cover design: Tyler Ottinger
Cover art: Shutterstock
Interior design: Maggie Urgo

PRINTED IN THE UNITED STATES OF AMERICA

# Introduction

Just north of Pocahontas, Arkansas, there is a beautiful bend in the road named Engelberg. The immigrant farmers who arrived there in the nineteenth century envisaged their native Switzerland in the hills and decided to make the area their home. It had been a rainy month the morning I set out to celebrate confirmation there, and before I left home the pastor called to report that the final leg of the road to Engelberg might be flooded. If I came upon a sign that indicated such was the case, I was to call a certain parishioner on his cellphone. He would direct me to Engelberg by another route.

Sure enough, as I turned down the road to Engelberg, I spotted an ominous orange sign announcing that the Fourche River had jumped its banks, the road was dangerously flooded, and all drivers should turn back. I called the parishioner for advice. He responded with an offhanded chuckle, "It's OK to drive right through the water, as long as you can see the yellow line in the middle of the road."

I said to myself: "I'm driving an SUV, and the parishioner is confident. Go for it." As I approached the flooded section of the road and realized it was not much more than a paved dirt levy, however, I began to have doubts. The wind was whipping the water into waves that licked the high door of my vehicle — but I could still see the yellow line. Cautiously, slowly, nervously, I made my way safely across the water.

I had planned to take the long way home that night, but the same confident parishioner offered to lead me back across the flooded road in his pickup. Off we went into the watery darkness, no less for the wear.

All of us use guideposts and road maps to help keep us clear of danger and on the right path: "As long as you can see the yellow line." "As long as the fuel indicator light doesn't come on." "As long as…" Each of us fills in the blank. Even if we don't always pay attention to our guideposts, we know we should, and we know instinctively what will happen if we ignore them.

The Advent/Christmas season reminds us that one criterion above all is worth remembering: "As long as you keep your eyes on Jesus."

Who of us does not need a regular time of silence and peace, a time to let the events and trials of life fall into perspective — Jesus' perspective? Who of us does not need him to guide us on his way, his star to enlighten our confusion, his gentle hand to nudge us along?

Advent offers a quiet opportunity to see the Lord Jesus as the only Light, the only Star, the only Guide. He, after all, is the Way. It is my prayer that these simple reflections help you keep your eyes fixed on him — and to discover anew that he has never taken his eyes off you.

*Archbishop J. Peter Sartain*

# The Lord is close at hand
# — and calms our fears

I'm embarrassed to say that I used to be afraid of Mr. Bingle. Each Christmas shopping season back in the 1950s, Lowenstein's department store featured the diminutive snowman puppet with a high-pitched voice that encouraged boys' and girls' excitement about the latest toys. For some reason he frightened me. Perhaps it was the movie about the Abominable Snowman I heard the older kids talking about. I didn't know what "abominable" meant, but it sounded ominous enough to keep me at a safe distance.

On Thanksgiving Day a few years ago, the Memphis, Tennesee, newspaper featured a story about Mr. Bingle, and one of my sisters reminded me how I used to hide when he appeared on television — as if I needed the reminder.

One Christmas, when one of my nephews was a toddler, I gave him a book about a baby monster who was unable to sleep at night because he kept having nightmares that a little boy was hiding under his bed. The baby monster's mom and dad helped him conquer his fear of going to sleep.

I, too, was afraid of going to sleep alone in my room at that age. The solution was to keep the door open so the hall light could shine near my bed, and I then could hear the television and the voices of family members. Not feeling alone any longer, I went fast asleep. It made me feel secure that someone was within earshot, even if no one was actually in the room with me. The family was near.

Most of us overcame unfounded childhood fears by learning that someone was close enough to make sure no harm would come to us. That someone was real, but the things we feared were not.

As we age, irrational fear still can have a way of unsettling us — the feeling of being utterly alone, wondering if anyone notices our plight; idle speculation run amuck, worrying that the unthinkable but unlikely could actually happen; memories of past mistakes replayed in our heads, painful "what ifs" gnawing at our consciences.

*Whatever the source of our apprehension — real or imagined — it somehow helps to know that someone is near.*

Not all anxieties are irrational, of course. We know from experience that life has its dangers and disappointments, its traps and tragedies. These are not phantoms of our imagination, and they can threaten our peace of mind.

Whatever the source of our apprehension — real or imagined — it somehow helps to know that someone is near. Having friends and family within earshot, experiencing their encouragement and support, our loads are lightened and we find strength to forge ahead.

In much the same way, but at a much more profound level, Advent teaches that Someone is indeed near.

"The reign of God is at hand!" John the Baptist announces in the Gospel of Matthew (see 3:1-3).

"Say to those whose hearts are frightened: Be strong, fear not! Here is your God, he comes with vindication . . . sorrow and mourning will flee," prophesies Isaiah (35:4,10).

"Make your hearts firm, for the coming of the Lord is at hand," writes James (5:8).

"Do not be afraid to take Mary as your wife," the angel tells the confused and anxious Joseph in a dream. "It is through the holy Spirit that this child has been conceived in her." Just as Isaiah had prophesied, reveals the angel, "The virgin shall be with child and bear a son, and they shall name him Emmanuel," a name which means "God is with us" (see Mt 1:20-23).

"Go and tell John what you hear and see," Jesus says to the followers of John the Baptist. "The blind regain their sight, the lame walk, the lepers are cleansed, the deaf hear, the dead are raised, and the poor have the good news proclaimed to them" (Mt 11:5).

What does the nearness of God mean for us?

It means that we are not now, and never will be, alone. It means that everything that causes us to fear — rational or irrational, fact or fiction — is under God's vigilant watch. It means that his plan is taking its course, even if we are not able to see it. It means there is no difficulty, no danger, no sin that Jesus has not overcome for us in his death and resurrection. It means that in him we conquer everything. It means there is no reason to be afraid.

But it also means that we must pay attention to his nearness. If the reign of God is at hand, if our God comes with vindication, if the coming of the Lord is at hand, if God is with us, if the evidence of God's presence is everywhere, then we should take notice — and our lives should be different than they would be if God were nowhere to be found.

It is not a matter that our behavior should be different out of fear, as kids in a classroom hush and quit their foolishness because the teacher is just outside the door. Far to the contrary, our changed behavior helps us see God, hear him, recognize him, and welcome him.

It was their attentiveness to the nearness of God that kept Mary and Joseph from hiding in fear and confusion when confronted with surprising (one might say irrational) circumstances, and it enabled them instead to place their lives trustingly in God's hands, saying, "Let all things come about according to your will."

# This Advent, break out of your routine

One autumn Sunday afternoon many years ago, I drove to my mom's house for a visit. As I pulled into her driveway, I heard my nieces and nephew playing in the backyard. Once inside, I looked out the kitchen window and saw them having fun in the fallen leaves.

One of my nieces caught a glimpse of me spying through the window. She stopped in her tracks and yelled to her sisters and brother, "Drop your leaves! Peter's here!" They did drop their leaves and ran inside to greet me, as if they had not seen me in years. Needless to say, it made me feel good that they were willing to drop everything, even a fun afternoon among the leaves, just to see me.

Years passed, and they turned their attention to other, more grown-up, interests. One day, I called my sister's house to speak with her. My leaf-dropping niece, by then in the eighth grade, answered the phone. The conversation went something like this:

"Hi, Katy, it's Peter. How ya doin'?"

"Good."

"What are you doing?"

"Talking to you."

"How's school?"

"It's okay."

"Is your mom there?"

"Yes."

"May I speak with her?"

"Mom, it's Peter" (almost as if to add, "…again").

I asked myself, "What happened to the excitement I used to hear when I called or visited?" I suppose it grew up; busied itself with homework, music, and relationships; and settled nicely into a routine.

Early Christians were excited about their new faith and the expectation of the return of the Lord Jesus. When his second coming was not as soon as they had expected, they settled into the routine of everyday living. Some simply returned to their former way of life, numb to the prospects that their Lord was going to come again.

As we begin Advent, we hear Jesus say that back in the days of Noah folks went about regular business right up to the day Noah entered the ark. "They did not know until the flood came and carried them all away" (Mt 24:39). He warns us that it will be the same with his second coming. "So will it be [also] at the coming of the Son of Man."

*It is easy to fall into a routine, forgetting that Jesus is with us and will come again. Perhaps this Advent we will reach beneath our routine — beneath even the routine of our anxieties — and discover anew who it is for whom we truly hunger.*

Jesus says, "You also must be prepared" (Mt 24:44). Salvation is not something off in the distant future, so far away that it makes no demands on us in the present. The Lord Jesus will come again, at an hour we least expect; but he is also present now, especially in the sacraments, in his word, in the poor, and in our prayer. Each moment holds out to us the promise of coming face to face with him.

It is easy to fall into a routine, forgetting that Jesus is with us and will come again.

Paul sums it up this way: "You know the time; it is the hour now for you to awake from sleep" (Rom 13:11). He reminds us to awaken from our routine and rekindle our excitement for the coming of the Lord.

Jesus says that preparedness for his coming involves the kind of careful watchfulness we would have when guarding our homes from intruders. Perhaps he would also point out that we are to be on the watch for his presence as we would be for the perfect gift for our most cherished friend.

Blessed John Henry Newman (1801–1890) wrote:

> Do you know the feeling … of expecting a friend, expecting him to come and he delays? Do you know what it is to be in unpleasant company, and to wish for the time to pass away, and the hour strike when you may be at liberty? Do you know what it is to be in anxiety lest something should happen which may happen or may not, or to be in suspense about some important event, which makes your heart beat when you are reminded of it, and of which you think the first thing in the morning?
>
> Do you know what it is to have a friend in a distant country, to expect news of him, and to wonder from day to day what he is now doing, and whether he is well?... To watch for Christ is a feeling such as these.
>
> He watches for Christ, who has a sensitive, eager, apprehensive mind; who is awake, alive, quick-sighted, zealous in seeking and honoring him; who looks out for him in all that happens, and who would not be surprised, who would not be over-agitated or overwhelmed, if he found that he was coming at once. (Sermon, "Watching," first published in 1838)

In the coming weeks, we will hear prophets and apostles rouse us to watchfulness. Their words arise from a hunger for God so deep that it is almost beyond telling, so intense and utterly personal that it consumes them. Perhaps this Advent we will reach beneath our routine — beneath even the routine of our anxieties — and discover anew who it is for whom we truly hunger. May we be ready to drop everything when we catch him spying us through the window.

# God comes — in every present moment

Just as we would never drive our car only by looking behind through the rearview mirror, so we would never drive only by looking ahead through binoculars. In either case, we would miss what is right before our eyes.

"All our life is a preparation for the present moment," writes Msgr. Massimo Camisasca, bishop of Reggio Emilia-Guastalla, Italy. That is a powerful and startling statement. He is suggesting that the present moment — each present moment — is full of powerful, life-changing possibilities for which God has prepared us through what has come before. Yesterday was preparation for today, today for tomorrow, tomorrow for the next tomorrow. All our life is preparation for the present moment, full of promise, full of the presence of God.

We are accustomed to regarding Advent as a time of waiting, of preparation, for both the feast of Christmas and the second coming of the Lord, and that is an important perspective. To arrive at the feast without having slowed ourselves down to ponder its meaning would be to sell Christmas short and deprive ourselves of its true gifts. To ignore Jesus' promise to return would be to let our hearts become drowsy and complacent (see Lk 21:34-36).

However, there is another aspect of Advent to which Msgr. Camisasca's words apply. Advent reminds us that God comes to us in the present moment, when we least expect it. Jesus makes this fact abundantly clear:

> Therefore, stay awake! For you do not know on which day your
> Lord will come. Be sure of this: if the master of the house had

known the hour of night when the thief was coming, he would have stayed awake and not let his house be broken into. So too, you also must be prepared, for at an hour you do not expect, the Son of Man will come. (Matthew 24:42-44)

The unpredictability of the Lord's coming is no reason for anxiety, as if the Lord would surprise us in an underhanded, scheming sort of way. Precisely because the present moment is that time in which the Lord could come, it contains a precious treasure, and all our life has prepared us for it. Staying awake, being prepared, means that we allow the hope springing from the promises of God to inspire and enliven the present moment with peace. Anxiety agitates and distracts us from the present moment and does not prepare us for anything.

Another tendency could be to consider God and the fulfillment of his promises as something "out there," far into the future. Thus we would consider today just one more step in that direction without any particular significance of its own. We might say to ourselves: "I am busy today. I can prepare tomorrow, for no one knows when the Lord will come. I see no signs of his coming today."

*Staying awake, being prepared, means that we allow the hope springing from the promises of God to inspire and enliven the present moment with peace. Anxiety agitates and distracts us from the present moment and does not prepare us for anything.*

None of what I have written assumes that we will always understand exactly how life up to now has prepared us for now — "God writes straight with crooked lines," according to an old Portuguese proverb. Perhaps we waste time, but God does not, and he finds a way to make profitable use even of those times when we stray.

The Gospel of Matthew begins with the genealogy of Jesus. In this way Matthew reveals the coming of Jesus as the climax of the history of Israel — the "coming" for which everything previous was preparation. To study "the book of the genealogy of Jesus Christ, the son of David, the son of Abraham" (Mt 1:1) is to see God's faithfulness in the midst of human wanderings.

Pope Emeritus Benedict XVI wrote in one of his homilies: "The genealogy with its light and dark figures, its successes and failures, shows us that God can write straight even on the crooked lines of our history. God allows us our freedom, and yet in our failures he can always find new paths for his love. God does not fail."

It is for this reason that Advent invites us neither to lament the past nor be anxious about the future, but to give today to God. Knowing that he has not wasted our past and that the future is securely in his hands, we can assume that we arrived at the present moment by his providence and that because Jesus is Emmanuel — God-with-us —.it is *now* that he comes to us. To be ready, to be prepared, is to know that God, in his love, has readied us and prepared us to receive him in the present moment. With quiet, peace-filled attention we will notice him. It is now, in the present moment, that we follow him.

# Keeping an inner diary: noticing signs of God's nearness

I have never kept a diary, though at the time of my ordination to the priesthood I was strongly encouraged to do so by Brother Randal Riede, a member of the Congregation of the Brothers of St. Francis Xavier (the Xaverian Brothers). His encouragement was not unique to me, for he offered it to all who would listen.

Librarian for the North American College for twenty-six years, to us students Brother Randal was friend, confidant, mentor, guide, and prodder. While tending efficiently to daily tasks, he kept one ear open for anyone who walked through the door, offering sensible advice from literature, history, the saints, and his native Kentucky. He was legendary for serving coffee and tea (neither of them especially good) and counsel (unfailingly reliable). I sat at his table almost daily.

*"To keep a kind of inner diary of good things would be a beautiful and healing task."*

In suggesting to most everyone to keep a diary, he was speaking from experience. For decades he had kept one himself, making time each night to record events and impressions of the day. We often wondered whether we had been the subjects of an entry.

I made several attempts to follow his advice but was never disciplined enough to persevere. I wish I had been. Although there will be no diary in my personal legacy, I try each day to do what Brother Randal did — to be attentive, to notice, to recognize that God is at work through the people and events I encounter moment by moment. I suppose I keep what might be called an "inner diary."

To tell the truth, I think everyone does. We take in what happens in the course of our waking hours, evaluate it, react to it, accept or reject it. We observe things good and bad, hear words kind and insensitive, think thoughts happy and gloomy. In my case, distractions and preoccupations often diminish my attentiveness, and I find myself having to reengage consciously with the present moment. Some of what we experience in the course of a day remains permanently etched in our inner diary, for good or for ill.

A few years ago I came across "An Advent Dialogue with the Sick," a reflection written by Pope Emeritus Benedict XVI when he was archbishop of Munich. He suggested:

> Perhaps we should try an experiment. Let us understand the individual events of the day as little signs God sends us. Let us not take note only of the annoying and unpleasant things; we should endeavor to see how often God lets us feel something of his love. To keep a kind of inner diary of good things would be a beautiful and healing task.

There could be no better Advent project than to keep "an inner diary of good things." I think Brother Randal would approve.

Theodore Ryken, founder of the Xaverian Brothers, once wrote that he tried to follow God's will in "the common, ordinary, unspectacular flow of everyday life." His insight was that the "common, ordinary, and unspectacular" matters to God, that he uses it to speak to us. Daily life, even when troublesome, always holds "something of his love" and is thus worthy of our attention.

In what would an inner diary of good things consist? Here I am not worried about appearing simplistic, because the simpler, the better. Such a diary would take note of:

The coffee that warmed me early this morning.

The psalm that caught my attention.

The coworker who greeted me with a smile though she is worried about her parents and kids.

The stranger who held the door when I was shopping.

The insightful comment that caused me to reconsider a hastily formed opinion.

The raspy cough that slowed me down and gave me a few hours of quiet.

The childhood photograph that reminded me how blessed I was in my family.

The joke that made me laugh.

The fallen leaves that beautifully display nature's course in God's design.

God's astounding forgiveness, through which he unhesitatingly receives me back when I have sinned.

A friend's forgiveness, which reveals his or her friendship with God.

The simple fact that God uses me for his purposes.

The realization that the smallest good deed combats the power of evil.

The impulse to call or write a family member or friend for no other reason than to say "hello" (for the impulse to love is a sign of God's presence).

The letter that said someone was thinking of me.

The fact that God is thinking of me.

The fact that God knows me through and through.

The fact that God desires my love. Yes, *my* love.

The list could be endless because God is with us always. Advent teaches us to take note that in the extraordinary grace of the Incarnation God took on the common, ordinary, and unspectacular, and it is most often there that we find him.

I think Brother Randal kept a diary because he did not want to forget the marks left on his life by God, family, and friends. I have no doubt that what fills its pages is sober, wise, clever, and funny, and that it shines with the goodness of daily living — with "something of his love." May our Advent inner diary also be filled to overflowing with good things. The Lord is near and will always be.

# Admitting our need for God

A priest friend from Missouri once worked diligently to map out his family tree, but eventually hit a brick wall. His records stopped with the couple that had come to this country more than one hundred years earlier from a little town in the Netherlands.

He decided to spend a summer vacation traveling to that town, armed with his incomplete family tree and the names of the immigrant couple. Arriving late one afternoon, he went straightaway to the town hall. When he mentioned the name of his ancestors, the people in the office recognized it immediately; and by the end of the evening he was sitting in the home of distant relatives. They, too, had been working on the family tree; and they, too, had come to a standstill at the precise place my friend had stopped. The two family trees fit hand in glove.

Advent brings us to the precise point where our Old Testament and New Testament family trees meet, the point of contact between our longing and God's fulfillment, when Mary visits Elizabeth (see Lk 1:39-44). John the Baptist, the last of the Old Testament prophets, meets the one whose way he has come to make ready. Even in Elizabeth's womb he recognizes the presence of the Messiah, and thus comes a moment in history when God's family tree of the Old Testament fit hand in glove with that of the New Testament.

Advent is a time for encounter between the old and the new, between promise and fulfillment, between our insufficiency and God's fullness. It's the season for recalling the perfect fit made possible as God poured forth his love in Jesus Christ. It's the opportunity for joyfully rediscovering our need for salvation.

Have you ever done your best, done all you had been taught and trained to do, only to find that life still had not met your expectations?

*Advent brings us to the precise point where our Old Testament and New Testament family trees meet, the point of contact between our longing and God's fulfillment.*

Have you ever tried to be the perfect husband, the perfect mother, the perfect physician, the perfect teacher, only to watch yourself blow it under the stress of the day?

Have you ever tried to take the Gospel seriously, wanting with all your might to follow God wholeheartedly, only to discover that you are just as capable of sin as ever?

Have you ever suffered from serious illness and felt powerless to heal yourself?

Have you ever had the feeling that even though everything in your life was going fine — family, job, or the social scene — there was still a deep vacuum which made you wonder what was missing?

Have you ever felt as if it were yourself against the world, that it was your duty to fight your own battles, brave every storm alone, conquer every challenge without help from anyone — only to admit eventually with embarrassment that you needed help, needed people, needed a shoulder to cry on?

Have you ever waited in what seemed like endless anticipation for God to show you the way?

Have you ever admitted that you need God?

These are the great questions of the Bible, the deep longing of the prophets, the persistent aching of the human heart. Advent is the time for us to savor these questions and come to the greatest admission of all: We cannot save ourselves. We need a Savior.

Throughout this season we hear the longing of the people of Israel for the Messiah, we hear John the Baptist telling us to be ready for his coming, and we celebrate his birth.

But how will we welcome him if we do not admit that we need a Savior, if we do not take time to search for him in humility and silent prayer?

There is probably no better way to prepare for Christmas than to admit our insufficiency, our weakness, our incapacity to save ourselves. In many ways this is what Advent is all about: preparing a way by recognizing that only God can fulfill us.

To admit our insufficiency is not a sign of defeat; to do so is a sign of welcome to the Savior. Jesus is ready — and desires — to come to us. Will we let him in?

The two great branches of God's family tree met the day the pregnant Mary greeted the pregnant Elizabeth. But these branches meet again and again, hand in glove with a perfect fit, each time you and I pray, "Come, Lord Jesus." As St. Augustine wrote in the fifth century, "You have made us for yourself, O Lord, and our hearts are restless until they rest in you."

A friend once told me that his youngest son, who had recently become an altar server, wanted to make sure he awoke on a particular morning to serve early Mass, so he slept in his clothes. When his dad went into his room at 5:45 a.m. to awaken him, he saw a sign on the wall with an arrow pointing to a glass of water on the nightstand. The sign read, "Please pour this on my head." He wanted to be sure he was awake, and ready.

John the Baptist appeared on the scene as the one about whom Isaiah had spoken: "A voice of one crying out in the desert: 'Prepare the way of the Lord, make straight his paths'" (Lk 3:4). God is about to pay the price of our ransom. Jesus Christ our hope is born! He has made us for himself, a perfect fit.

# Grief can help unite us with Advent readings

The early years of the Sartain family are generously chronicled in a series of home movies, the first of which were taken before I was born. My father loved gadgets, and as home movie cameras became available, he followed us kids with great interest, recording our every move with enthusiasm. Bright light was a necessity for these pioneering cameras, and indoors he used a hand-held bank of floodlights so blinding that we squinted painfully as the film rolled — not exactly the best way to produce a natural pose.

For many years, my mother kept canisters containing these old movies (many of them labeled in grease pencil) in a metal cabinet in her bedroom closet. The movies produced before I was born feature fairly generic titles: "Kids At Zoo," "Kids At Grandma's," etc. But several canisters stand out with such titles as "Peter On Slide" and — my personal favorite — "Our Son." When I was born — the fifth child and first son — my father figured the event deserved special recognition.

Many years ago, one of my sisters transferred some of the movies to videotape and gave them to the rest of us as Christmas gifts. I followed suit several years later with the remainder and added a soundtrack composed mostly of theme songs from television shows of the 1950s and '60s. I took great pains to emphasize my first appearance on the screen. "Peter Learns To Walk" features Handel's "Hallelujah Chorus" and Aaron Copland's "Fanfare for the Common Man." The temptation was too hard to resist.

I think my sister and I had the same objective: to preserve part of our family history, and in a certain sense to do so in the spirit of my father, who loved this kind of project and first made it possible. The fact that the project was destined to be a Christmas gift added another layer of significance, for Christmas celebrations are part of every family history.

This time of year I am keenly aware of families who are celebrating the holidays for the first time without a loved one who has recently died. The grieving process is almost always heightened during the holidays — precisely because holidays bring back family memories — and navigating these days can require special strength and ingenuity.

Many of us heap loads of expectations on the holidays — what they should be like, how we should feel, where we should be, who should be there with us. But circumstances often change, and holidays can become heavy if we force unrealistic expectations into changed circumstances. If those expectations are not met, many people end up sorely disappointed.

When we have recently lost a loved one, holidays can be particularly hard to handle and cause us to turn inward even though surrounded by friends and family. At times like these it is helpful to give deliberate direction to our naturally inward gaze. Let me tell you what I mean.

The inward orientation of grief offers a prime opportunity to deepen one's understanding of the meaning of the holidays. For example, Thanksgiving Day can be re-enlivened as a day of gratitude for blessings big and small, most especially perhaps for the blessing of the one who has died. A reflective attitude gives us the opportunity to thank God for the blessings our loved one brought us and helps us remember other blessings that may have been forgotten as in a closet for years. Giving thanks strengthens our hope and gives us courage, because it brings to mind friends and loved ones who have constantly streamed through our lives from the beginning.

Those who are grieving can experience the Christmas mystery in a new and wonderful way. The very fact that they are grieving gives them a heightened understanding of themes that appear in the Scriptures of Advent and Christmas. Who better than they can grasp the longing of the people of Israel? Or the expectation of the world to come, when all will be reunited in Christ? Or the poverty of spirit shown by the Virgin Mary, who despite the troubling questions passing through her mind accepted God's will with an open heart, who heard Simeon predict that one day her heart would feel as though it had been pierced by a sword?

> *Those who are grieving can experience the Christmas mystery in a new and wonderful way.... Who better than they can grasp the longing of the people of Israel? Or the expectation of the world to come, when all will be reunited in Christ? Or the poverty of spirit shown by the Virgin Mary?*

Who better than they can comprehend the sinking fear that arises upon hearing painful news, such as Joseph and Mary felt when they suddenly discovered on their way home from Jerusalem that their son was lost? Or what St. Paul described as the inward groaning of all creation as it awaits redemption? Or the frightening void exposed by grief that can be filled only by God himself? Grieving people understand these things better than most.

Though such "first holidays" may appear to be the end of holidays as we knew them, they can occasion a deepening of our appreciation of the Christian mystery and the reason we need Jesus Christ, who came to destroy death forever.

May God bless you who have said goodbye to your loved ones in recent years, and may their passing through your hearts during the holidays be an occasion for gratitude and strengthened faith. May your longing for them be transformed into a prayer of longing for the Savior. I assure you, God listens attentively to such prayers that rise to him out of our depths.

# What we can learn from Simeon and Anna

When Jesus was first brought to the Temple by his parents, how did Simeon and Anna know he was the One for whom they had been waiting?

Joseph and Mary were devout Jews who faithfully observed the Law of Moses. St. Luke writes that they came to the Temple when Jesus was forty days old for the ritual purification of Mary after childbirth and the consecration of their firstborn to the Lord. They made the symbolic offering prescribed for the poor. It was there that they met two prayerful children of Israel, Simeon and Anna.

Simeon and Anna were part of the *anawim*, God's poor, who are mentioned countless times in the Old Testament. The *anawim* were objects of God's tender love and care, examples of humility and generosity, who trusted not in their own resources but solely on the providence of God. Unshaken in faith despite the misfortunes that had befallen them, they were examples to others who struggled to keep their sights on the Lord.

Simeon was "righteous and devout, awaiting the consolation of Israel, and the holy Spirit was upon him. It had been revealed to him by the holy Spirit that he should not see death before he had seen the Messiah of the Lord" (Lk 2:25-26).

Anna was eighty-four, a widow most of her life. "She never left the temple, but worshiped night and day with fasting and prayer" (Lk 2:37).

I am certain it is fair to say that everyone knew Simeon and Anna, because they were always in the Temple. Having rooted themselves deep in the hopes of Israel, they never left the house of God. "Why would we be anywhere else?" they must have thought. "The Messiah is coming!"

Both of them instantly recognized Jesus as the One for whom they had been waiting. Simeon took the baby in his arms and praised God, declaring that he could now die in peace because he had seen the salvation promised by the Lord (see Lk 2:29-32). Anna saw the baby, gave thanks to God, and began speaking about him to "all who were awaiting the redemption of Jerusalem" (v. 38).

How did they know he was the One? Because he was the focus of their waiting.

Simeon and Anna could have focused on waiting for a solution to their problems. Since they were poor, I am sure they had concerns about food, clothing, and shelter. Were they lonely, and did they pray for companionship? Did others look at them suspiciously, snickering at their permanent presence in the Temple? As a widow, Anna was particularly vulnerable. Who was taking care of her in her old age? Knowing that he would not die until he saw the Messiah, did Simeon worry that his creaking joints and unsteady gait would get the best of him in the meantime?

*Advent is a time for us to take up the spirit of Simeon and Anna. It is easy to focus energy and attention exclusively on seeking answers to our prayers, but to do so can actually be another way of focusing on ourselves. Advent calls us to move our focus away from the answers we await and toward the One who answers every prayer.*

They had plenty to pray about, plenty to ask, plenty of answers to wait for. Yet they waited only for the Lord. It is precisely here that we find the blessedness of their situation and the reason for the clarity of their insight: they were not looking for an answer or a solution, but for the Messiah.

Advent is a time for us to take up the spirit of Simeon and Anna. It is easy to focus energy and attention exclusively on seeking answers to our prayers, but to do so can actually be another way of focusing on ourselves. Advent calls us to move our focus away from the answers we await and toward the One who answers every prayer. It can be frightening to take such a leap, but in reality it is very liberating to do so.

Simeon and Anna recognized the Savior when he was brought to the Temple because it was he for whom they looked, and only he. Their needs were great, and I doubt they were bashful in prayer. They must have poured out their hearts to God time and again. Their knees must have been calloused and achy from all the praying. But they had let go of looking for answers in favor of relying, simply and hopefully, on God.

In a sense, Advent is a time to taste heaven. We will know then, beyond a shadow of a doubt, who the Messiah is. Then, there will be no more waiting, no prayers to be answered. Then, there will be only God, the One on whom we have always depended for everything, even when we frantically looked elsewhere for answers. In heaven, we will pray for our loved ones who are still in this life, and our prayer will be something like this: "Lord, may she turn to you. Lord, may he rely on you. Lord, may they recognize you."

This Advent, may the words of Psalm 62:6-9 be our dearest prayer:

> In God alone be at rest, my soul;
> for my hope comes from him.
> He alone is my rock, my stronghold,
> My fortress: I stand firm.

> In God is my safety and glory,
> The rock of my strength.

Take refuge in God all you people,
Trust him at all times.

Pour out your hearts before him.
For God is our refuge.

(From *Benedictine Daily Prayer: A Short Breviary*)

# In Jesus, I have everything

What do I need for Christmas?

Perhaps that is the question I should ask every year as Advent begins. It is an interesting question, because it calls me to a change of perspective during a season of wishes and gift lists. Even as folks ask me what I want for Christmas, I should be asking myself what it is I *need* for Christmas.

It is also an interesting question, however, because sacred Scripture proclaims that in Jesus I already have everything I need. "Blessed be the God and Father of our Lord Jesus Christ, who has blessed us in Christ with every spiritual blessing in the heavens" (Eph 1:3). "His divine power has bestowed on us everything that makes for life and devotion, through the knowledge of him who called us by his own glory and power" (2 Pt 1:3). "In times past, God spoke in partial and various ways to our ancestors through the prophets; in these last days, he spoke to us through a son . . . through whom he created the universe" (Heb 1:1-2).

If in Jesus I have already received "every spiritual blessing in the heavens," "everything that makes for life," and a Son "through whom he created the universe," what more could I want or need?

It seems to me that too often we settle for skimming the surface of our relationship with Jesus, unwittingly assuming that it is possible to exhaust the potential of one stage of that relationship and move on to the next. Sadly, perhaps we sometimes suspect that Jesus is not everything and go looking elsewhere for fulfillment, as if there are gaps to fill. Or maybe we wonder if there is something God is holding back from us until he sees fit to reveal it. Will there be another word from God some day?

*I need strength to love more courageously, discipline to pray more devotedly.*

Commenting on the passage from Hebrews I quoted above, St. John of the Cross recognized that it is not uncommon for us to ask God for "more," for another word, as if Jesus is not enough. He wrote:

> In giving us his Son, his only Word (for he possesses no other), he spoke everything to us at once in this sole Word — and he has no more to say . . . because what he spoke before in the prophets in parts, he has now spoken all at once by giving us the All Who is His Son. Any person questioning God or desiring some vision or revelation would be guilty not only of foolish behavior but also of offending him, by not fixing his eyes entirely upon Christ and by living with the desire for some other novelty. (*The Ascent of Mount Carmel*, 2, 22, 3-5)

If in Christ the Father has given everything — said everything — and there will be no other word than he, what could I possibly need for Christmas?

I need the gift of depth, that I might plumb the inexhaustible gift who is Jesus my Lord. I need a slower pace to savor the richness of the Gospel, patience to let go of the desire for quick fixes to my problems. I need boldness to travel trustingly the long road ahead, contrition for my failure to live a truly Christian life. I need strength to love more courageously, discipline to pray more devotedly. I need generosity to swallow my stinginess, humility to soften my pride, gratitude to overturn my thanklessness, grace to conquer my self-assurance. I need to admit that I need a Savior.

Advent is the season to go deep so that we might appreciate even more what God has given us in his Son. We will never respond properly to Our Lord if we remain on the surface. We will never appreciate his gifts until we put them to use. We will never understand the Gospel unless we try to live it. We will never know Jesus unless we take everything we have placed ahead of him and put it under him, ready to abandon it if in his light we see it to be false or harmful.

I always enjoy the Scripture readings for Advent, because we hear the prophets put words to the people's hunger for a Savior and proclaim God's fiery, but patient, encouragement. "Oh, that you would rend the heavens and come down, / with the mountains quaking before you, / . . . While you worked awesome deeds we could not hope for, / such as had not been heard of from of old. / No ear has ever heard, no eye ever seen, / any God but you / working such deeds for those who wait for him" (Is 63:19—64:3).

The wonderful mystery of Advent is that, in Jesus, God has rent open the heavens, done awesome deeds we could never have imagined, revealed what eye could not hope to see, spoken the Word that says it all. The task for you and me is to prepare a place deep within, a humble stable at our very core where Jesus will be born in us anew. With humble hearts let us admit this Advent that we have only begun to know him.

> Give me Jesus, give me Jesus.
> You may have all the world
> but give me Jesus.
> (*Traditional African-American spiritual*)

# Holding back nothing from God

What will I give God for Christmas? I have suggested that a good Advent question would be, "What do I need for Christmas?" Its corollary is, "What will I give God for Christmas?"

We spend a great deal of time each year deciding what to buy loved ones for Christmas, and while it is easy to decide on the right gift for some, when it comes to others we may be faced with a challenge. What do they want? What do they need? Which gift will fit each personality? Which gift will express the bond we feel with that person? Which gift will please our family, our friends? To the one who has everything, or to the one who has little but asks for nothing, what do we give?

Most of us have experienced disappointment at gifts received, not received, and altogether forgotten. Perhaps we were not given the gift we had hoped for; perhaps we knew by the look on the face of the one receiving our gift that we had fallen short. Expectations — ours and theirs — can spoil everything.

It is entirely possible that Jesus' friends, especially those closest to him, gave him gifts — or at least wanted to. They probably discussed among themselves what would please him, what he needed, what he should have, what they wanted him to have. I'll bet he rolled his eyes and smiled. And I'll bet he received every gift with gratitude. As with us, their motives were perhaps mixed — the Gospels don't shy from exposing the divided hearts of the disciples — but even in their lack of understanding they still wanted to please their Lord, and he understood.

In our gift-giving we often focus too much on expectations and reciprocity, and not enough on the depth of the gift, the depth of the love from which it springs. Our occasional disappointment both in what we receive and what we perceive in the faces of those to whom we have given speaks volumes about what lies beneath. To an extent, all of us must admit, it's all about "me." As embarrassing as such a realization might be, it should not surprise us, nor should it make us sad. We can simply roll our eyes — at ourselves — then give and receive each gift with gratitude.

*With all his heart he wants us to experience the joy that comes to those who give themselves to him, just as he gave himself for us.*

Discipleship is about making myself less the center of things and making Christ the true center. That means I will continually be getting out of the way to let him in. I will continually be giving back to him the throne where my feelings and expectations have stolen center stage.

A question naturally arises. Does Christ want to be the center of our lives out of a kind of divine pride, a need to receive adulation and attention? Does he think so little of us that he wants us to remain on the sidelines as mere spectators to his wonders?

To the contrary: He desires us at the center with him, in him, and for him. With all his heart he wants us to experience the joy that comes to those who give themselves to him, just as he gave himself for us. He knows well the sadness and infuriating frustration that awaits those who reject him.

So what do we give to the One who has everything and is everything, the One who is the center and goal, the One who meets every expectation?

Jesus gave us more than a hint one day in the Temple as he and his disciples watched folks putting contributions in the coffers.

"When he looked up he saw some wealthy people putting their offerings into the treasury and he noticed a poor widow putting in two small coins. He said, 'I tell you truly, this poor widow put in more than all the rest; for those others have all made offerings from their surplus wealth, but she, from her poverty, has offered her whole livelihood'" (Lk 21:1-4).

The point here is not about amounts, but about the depth, intention, and quality of the gift. After all, God, who has everything, does not need our gifts. The poor widow had little. The little she had was her everything, but she gave it all. In offering "her whole livelihood" she held nothing back from God. We will never match the quantity of the gift God has given us in his Son, but we can respond to the gift in kind by giving ourselves to him, entirely.

What will I give God for Christmas? How about something I have refused to give him until now?

# Jesus' humility was a bright star to guide our way

When I think of the night Jesus was born, I like to imagine it as cold and crisp, stars glimmering brightly in a clear sky like candles in the hands of a thousand vigilant pilgrims. Goats and sheep shifted sleepily in their pens, while the occasional bark of a dog echoed off the hills, followed by the annoyed "Shush!" of its master. A breeze spread the lingering aroma of suppers cooked over smoldering hearths and campfires.

Joseph took a full, deep breath, then sighed in relief and wonder. I wonder if Mary was hungry. Their baby's full-throated cries pierced the evening's still, and the dog howled. Mary and Joseph smiled. Hanging like a huge painting on the night sky was the moon, which somehow seemed much closer than usual, its mysterious, distant features clearly discernible.

That night the moon was a lamp so bright that travelers could have effortlessly found their way down the crude roads by its light. It would have been easy to forget that it was not a star, that it simply reflected the extraordinary light of the hidden sun.

As I picture the first Christmas, I like to think that the brightness of the moon that night did not come from the sun. Instead, it came from the Savior, whose glory illumined the heavens, shining on the moon and radiating far past it. The true light of the world had come. In his homily for the closing of the Holy Door at the beginning of 2001, and again in his apostolic letter *Novo Millennio Ineunte* ("At the Beginning of the New Millennium"), St. John Paul recalled a favorite ancient image of the Church:

The theology of the Fathers loved to speak of the Church as *mysterium lunae* ["the mystery of the moon"], in order to emphasize that, like the moon, she shines not with her own light, but reflects Christ, who is her Sun. (3)

The night Jesus Christ was born, the reflected light of the sun paled in comparison to the light shining from a stable in Bethlehem. Though imperceptible to shepherds watching their flocks, it was seen by angels, who sang God's praises.

The Son of God, through whom all things came to be, had taken on flesh and blood, and the prayers of the ages were answered.

*Who could have guessed that we would share in the mystery, that we would be called to reflect the glory of the Son of God and draw others to him?*

Who would have thought that God could become so fragile, so small, so helpless? Who could have guessed that we would share in the mystery, that we would be called to reflect the glory of the Son of God and draw others to him?

Who could have known that humility would be the brightest light of all?

It had been a long journey just for the census, a long and worrisome day looking for lodging and a safe place to give birth.

Joseph lovingly admired his son and pondered the trip home, wondering when Mary would feel well enough to travel again.

He tried his best to stay awake with her, because he did not want to miss a thing, especially should she have any need. But crouched against the gate of the stall, his arm and warm cloak around her shoulders and his head against hers, his eyelids grew heavy, and he fell asleep.

# Will you feed, shelter, and welcome Jesus?

Since no one would take the poor travelers in for the night (they probably had no money, and she looked as if she would give birth at any moment, and it would be just too much of an inconvenience at such a busy time as the census), God set his Christmas table in a trough used to feed animals. Little did anyone know that stingy night that God's was to be a lavish banquet of choice food, a feast of endless abundance.

"If only we had known," the innkeepers might have said later, "we would have provided a proper room for them, and a nourishing meal." But they did not, and still there is enough food forever, and room for all.

They asked very little, this weary pair, and finally someone agreed to their simple requests: just a spot out back away from the wind, among the animals would be just fine, we'll be no trouble — and, yes, it seems the baby will come very soon — don't worry, we have food in our sacks, and blankets, too, just a place to rest and wait, we'll pay for some hay and water for the donkey, thank you for your kindness. Shalom, good night to you as well.

And there he was born, the one through whom all things came to be. St. Luke hopes we take note that this happened in a town whose name means "house of bread," and that Jesus was placed in a manger where creatures come to feed. He needed next to nothing, this little one who would one day give everything for us.

A fifth-century song for Christmas morning (*A solis ortus cardine*) captured the contrast: "The blessed maker of the world assumed a servant's form.... He deigned to have hay for a bed, and did not refuse the shelter of a manger. He does not suffer even a bird to hunger, and yet he was fed with a little milk." He provides the world its food, but is content with just a little for himself.

Soon strangers from the East brought gifts to the child, sensing by God's hidden wisdom that something earthshaking was afoot. They left their riches at his feet, but left with more than they had brought. Did they know whom they were visiting? One thing is certain: by grace they were changed on their star-crossed journey to the manger. St. Matthew means more than geography when he reports that they went back to their own country "by another way."

The child grew in wisdom, age, and grace. Still asking little or nothing, he gave everything to the poor and confused, the forsaken and lost, the stingy and ungrateful. They sought him out by the thousands. "I am the bread of life," he would tell them. "No one who comes to me will ever be hungry."

*The truth is, we have the chance to recognize and welcome him, to feed him and shelter him, every day.*

He would prove his love to the end; by the end he suffered on the cross. A soldier pierced him with a lance, and from his side sprang a fountain of blood and water. Having given his body and blood for us, the banquet was eternally set — the only banquet we would ever need, the Eucharist we share even today, and will forever.

He is our brother (flesh of our flesh), our food (satisfying Word and Precious Body and Blood), our Savior (God from all ages, our origin and destiny). Will we feed on him? That is the invitation of Christmas.

But there is another invitation, too: Will we feed him? Will we bring him our gifts? After all, he asks so little.

The truth is, we have the chance to recognize and welcome him, to feed him and shelter him, every day. Pope John Paul I, who served as pontiff for just 33 days in 1978, once wrote that parents, by caring for their children, honor Jesus: "Husbands and wives are themselves Magi, who deposit their gifts at the foot of that cradle every day: privations, anxieties, nightlong vigils, detachment. They receive other gifts in return, new impulses to live and become holy, a joy purified by sacrifice, the renewal of their mutual affection, and a fuller communion of souls."

That is the way he intended it to be: that we would let him feed us, and filled with him we would feed the world. Learning to love as he loved, we would find how rich is his banquet, how inexhaustible his generous love. Whether mothers or fathers, sons or daughters, priests or religious, nurses or teachers, or leaders of nations, that is the way he intends it to be. We who have the privilege of knowing who he is — unlike the miserly innkeepers of the first Christmas — are to let him in. He will feed us, and we will become food ourselves.

On that night, when no one was in any mood to take poor strangers in, God poured out his heart to us, giving us what was most precious to him, his only Son. We are Magi, too, and lay gifts at his feet every time we love as he loved.

May we know him in prayer, in sacrament, in love, in daily life. He asks so little, and gives us everything.

# Made by Love, for love

Some friends once confided in me before the birth of their second child that they worried that when she was born they would not be able to love her as much as they did their first child. They said, "We love Molly so much that we don't see how we could ever love another child so completely." It wasn't a question of not wanting another child — they were excited beyond words that she was on the way. They were afraid that somehow their store of love had already been given away, and they didn't want to shortchange the baby soon to be born.

They knew that the most important gift they would give their children was their love, and so they asked themselves: "Is it possible to give yourself completely to *every* child? Is it possible to love in such a way and to such a degree that one's love never runs out, that one's love is never exhausted?"

 *We know intuitively, from the tips of our toes to the tops of our heads, that, ultimately, everything is about love.*

The day Emily was born, they forgot they had once fretted over their capacity to love. They did not love Molly any less because Emily was now part of the family, and, in fact, they realized right away that in the blink of an eye their capacity to give and receive love had expanded far beyond their hopes. Seeing Molly's boundless love for her new little sister, they also marveled as *her* capacity to love grew, too.

My friends knew that the most important gift they would give their children was their love, because their love is the deepest expression of who they are. To love means not to give *something*, but to give *myself*. And, most importantly of all, to love means to *become myself completely.*

There is an intuition shared by all of us through which we know deep within that everything is about love, that everything is resolved in love. It is an intuition sometimes clouded and blurred by suffering, sadness, confusion, doubt, sin, selfishness, and the condition of the world itself. Ironically, even such clouds prove the intuition true. The very fact that my friends worried about not having enough love was a sign that they did! It was love already within them that was breaking out to grow their family.

We know intuitively, from the tips of our toes to the tops of our heads, that, ultimately, everything is about love. We know intuitively, from the tips of our toes to the tops of our heads, that we were made for love and that nothing else will fulfill us or make us whole.

Love is not a commodity to be bought and sold or a concept to be hammered out in endless discussion. It is not an idea to be debated or a method to achieve a goal. To use St. Paul's words, to talk of love without loving is to be nothing more than a noisy gong or a clanging cymbal. To be love, it must be lived.

During the Christmas season we give thanks that God's love for us is so great that it burst forth on earth, in flesh and blood, in his Son Jesus. "God so loved the world that he gave his only Son," the Evangelist John wrote (3:16). But we must also recognize that we ourselves are expressions of God's love, we are proofs that God is Love! We were made by Love, for love.

God is no noisy gong or clanging cymbal, and he would not stop at anything to tell us, the ones he loves, how much he loves us. He wanted us to see with our eyes and hear with our ears and touch his love with our hands, so he sent his Son in flesh and blood. Not only that: His Son was born where even the least could come see him, because he was born as one of them.

Shepherds heard the news and worshiped him long before kings and wise men.

Every once in a while, we might wonder: "I know God's love is great, and I believe that he sent his Son among us as Savior. But does God have enough love left for *me*? Am I, too, the object of his favor?"

Prophets and angels made it very clear that the Savior has come for *us*. The one who created us and loves us into life at every moment sent his Son, that our love might expand in him, and so that we might know from the tips of our toes to the tops of our heads that we are loved by him.

In the twelfth century, a French monk by the name of William of St. Thierry composed a prayer that captures the meaning of Christmas: "[O God], you first loved us so that we might love you — not because you needed our love, but because we could not be what you created us to be, except by loving you."

If love had its origin in us, it would indeed be limited, and we would have reason to fear that there would not be enough to go around. But because all love has its origin in God, and because he shares his love with us completely, the only limit is set by our selfishness. May we see and hear and touch God's love. May we love him in return, that we might be what he created us to be. Loving him, our love will expand beyond our deepest hopes.

# News of Christ's birth started
## as a rumor that spread

A rumor does not have to be a bad thing.
I am referring to the kind of excitement and speculation that erupt when potentially good news begins to spread. "Have you heard she may be coming home for Christmas?" "Did you know he's a finalist for the scholarship?" "Someone told me her cancer may be in remission!" "I saw them speaking and smiling the other day — could that mean they are reconciled?"

Word passes from one to another — a word of hope and anticipation, a word spread not because it is scandalous but because it is good. The crescendo increases as more and more folks are in on it; and though nothing yet has come to pass, just the thought builds good will, brings us together, and sets us to thinking generous thoughts.

"Could that be?" we might say. "Wouldn't that be wonderful? I hope it's true!" The word is so full of hope that we are surprised when someone discounts it or doesn't join in the excitement.

As Jesus began his public ministry, the good news of his preaching and accomplishments traveled like wildfire, and in those whose hearts were open wondrous speculation began.

Though rumors about Jesus were nothing new, their effect on others was unpredictable. In fact, it had been a rumor that brought together astrologers from the East, King Herod, chief priests, and scribes.

Three foreigners were in town inquiring about a star and a newborn king for the Jews. Worried, Herod consulted the experts.

"What does Scripture say about where your Messiah will be born?" he queried. "Bethlehem of Judea," they answered. Then, feigning intimate confidence in the Magi, he suggested they follow the star, find the new king, and bring back news of his location.

> *"Although the scribes could explain where the Messiah should be born, they remained quite unperturbed in Jerusalem. Similarly, we may know the whole of Christianity, yet make no movement."*

Off they went, enlightened by Scripture, ambassadors now of Herod himself. And finding Mary, Joseph, and the child, they believed; but it was revealed to them in a dream to avoid the duplicitous Herod, so they traveled home by another way, guided no longer by a star but by the Light of the World.

This was a confusing turn of events, to say the least. Pagan astrologers, acting on rumor and inspiration, left home and family to look for a Messiah. Put on the right track by experts, their unwitting search for faith ended in triumph. But the experts, who believed in both Scripture and God's promise of a Messiah, were indifferent to the rumor and did not budge. They held the key, but did not turn it.

Danish philosopher Søren Kierkegaard (1813-1855) wrote:

> Although the scribes could explain where the Messiah should be born, they remained quite unperturbed in Jerusalem. They did not accompany the Wise Men to seek him. Similarly, we may know the whole of Christianity, yet make no movement. The power that moved heaven and earth leaves us completely unmoved.

What a difference! The three kings had only a rumor to go by. But it moved them to make that long journey. What a vexation it must have been for the kings, that the scribes who gave them the news they wanted remained in Jerusalem!

Rumors about the birth of a new king were enough to stir the astrologers to the star-lit desert roads, but soon there was no longer any rumor for them. Matthew reports that they went back to their own country "by another way." Nothing would ever be the same again, now that they knew the truth.

Preaching to fourth-century catechumens, St. Cyril of Jerusalem remarked:

> The Incarnation was not merely a rumor or something men imagined; it took place in very truth. The Word did not pass through the Virgin as through a channel but was really made flesh out of her body; he really ate as we ate, and drank as we drink. For if his assumption of human nature had been only a pretense, so would our salvation be only a pretense.

Not a rumor at all, it turned out, but the Eternal Truth. He is not the kind of news to treat casually: he is the star that guides, the power that moves heaven and earth, the "rumor" to take to heart, as did the Virgin Mary. For he did not pass through her but became flesh in her. In a sense it was the same for the nomadic Magi: the good news that is Jesus did not pass through them as rumor but took flesh and remained in them. So may it be this year for you and me.